Published by
Tim Fieldstead Photography

first edition

ISBN 978-0-9576820-0-9

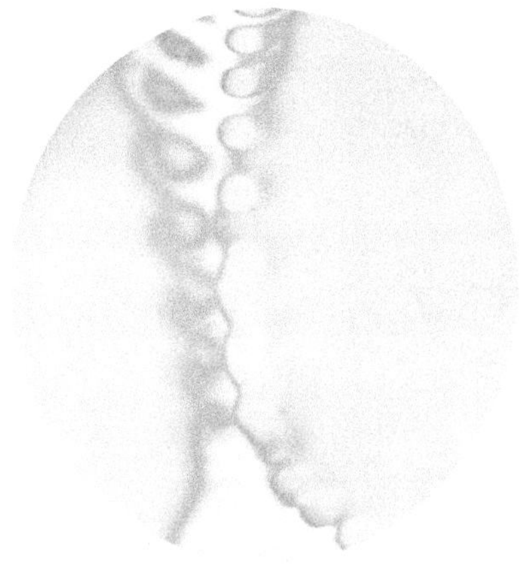

An exploration of those things that make me smile

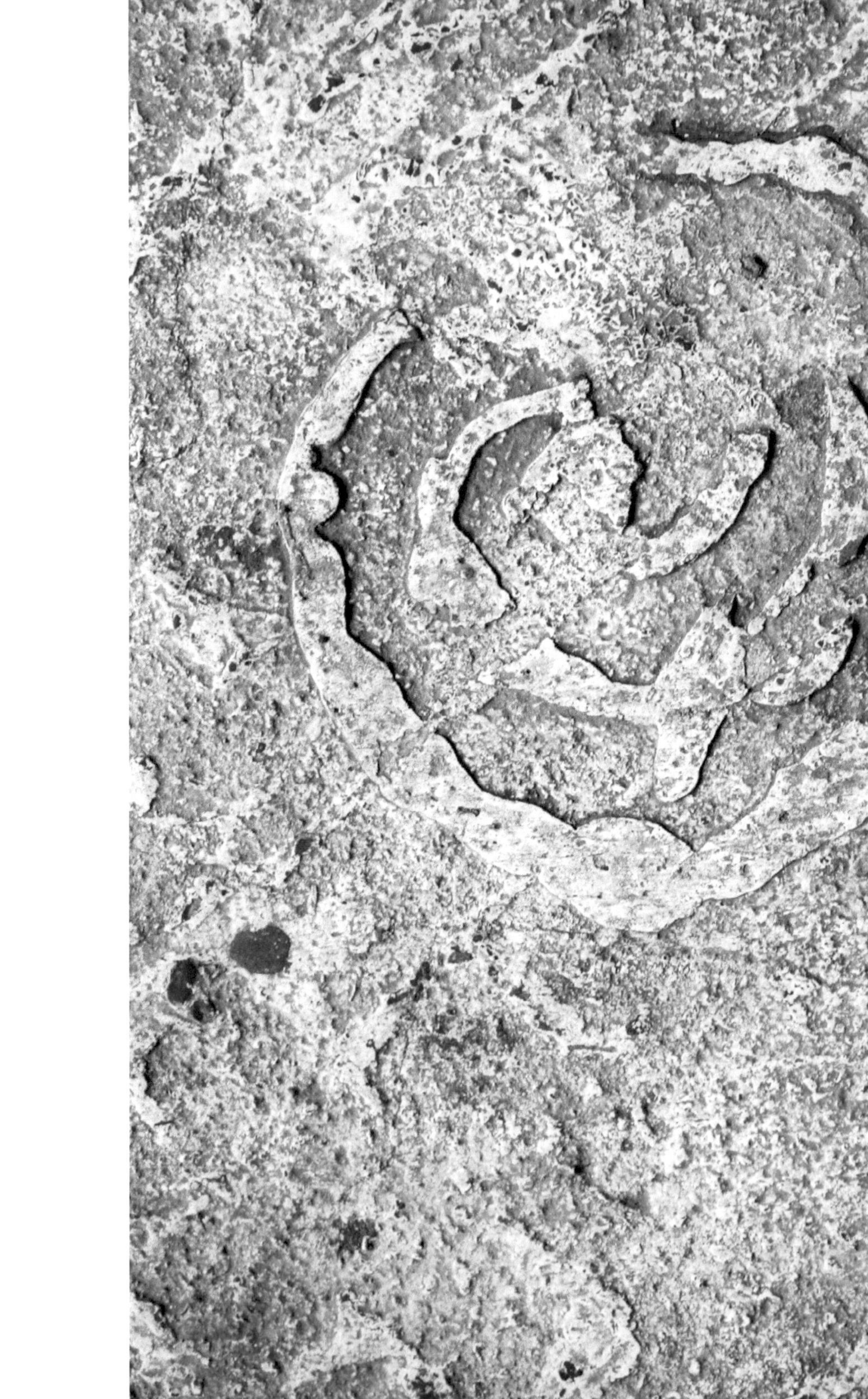

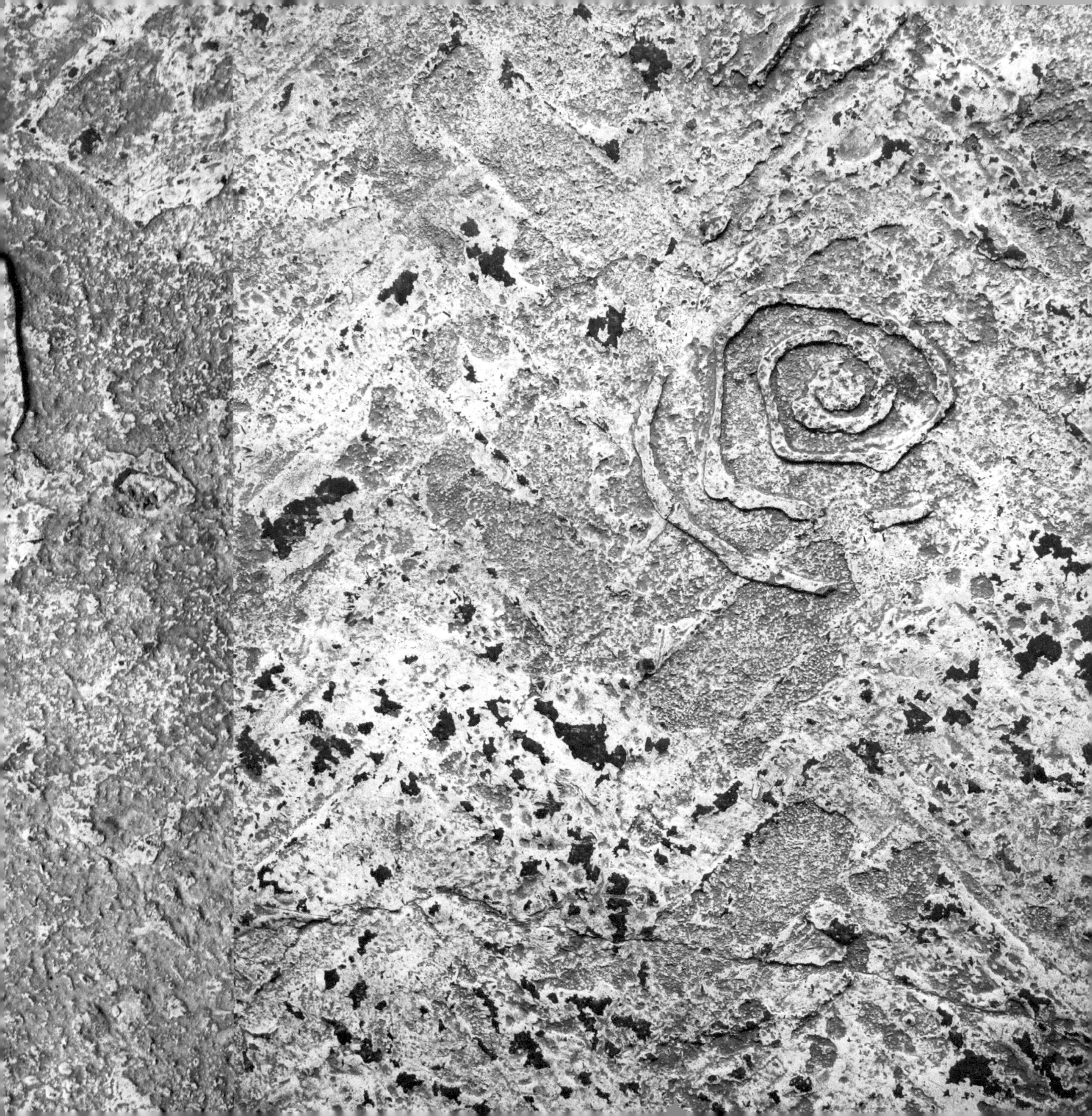

The texture of things always
catches my eye

How to capture it is a constant
challenge, which I enjoy everyday

*Experimenting with contrasts
always presents new possibilities
and directions to travel*

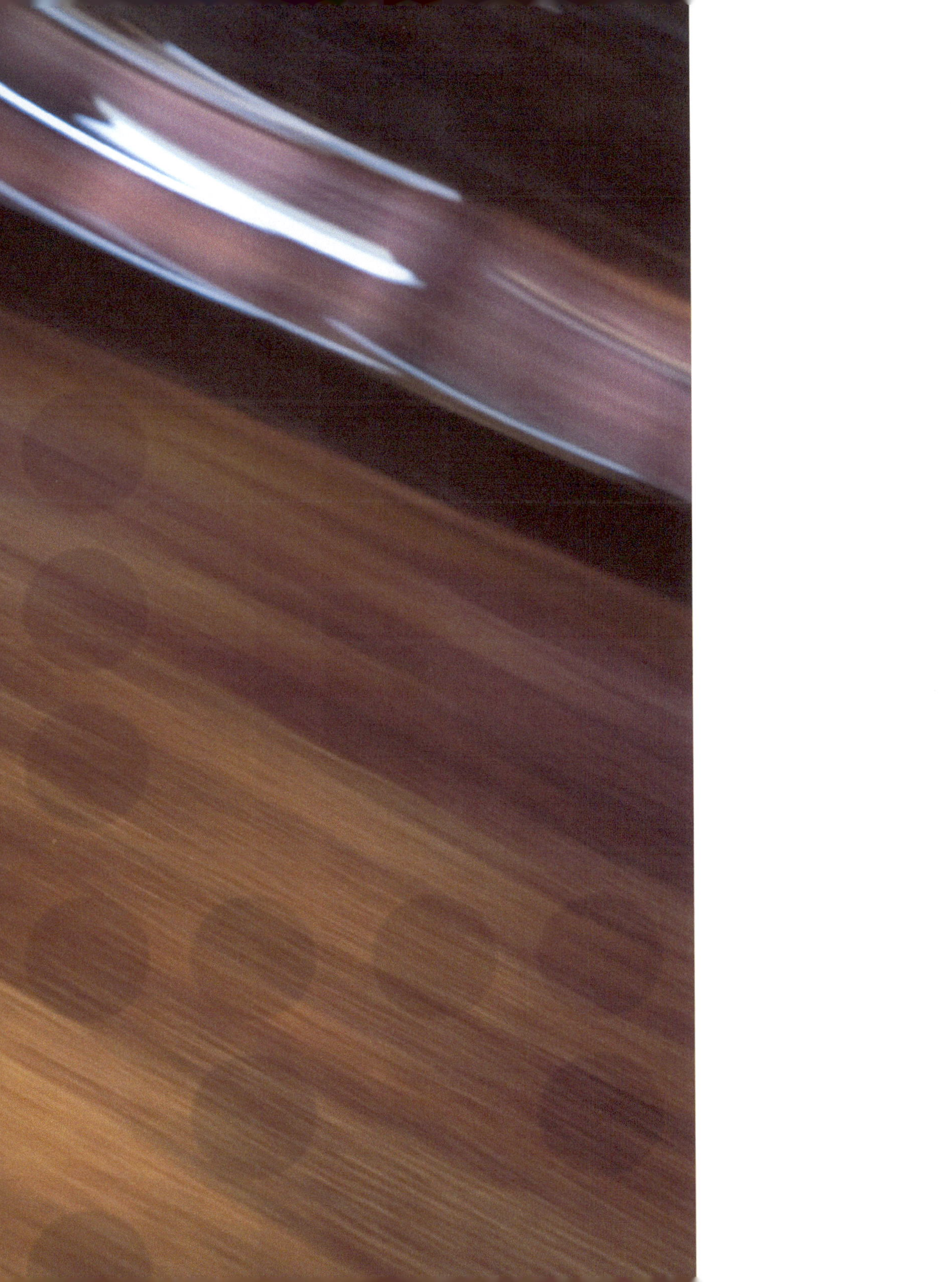

Challenging the everyday to be exciting

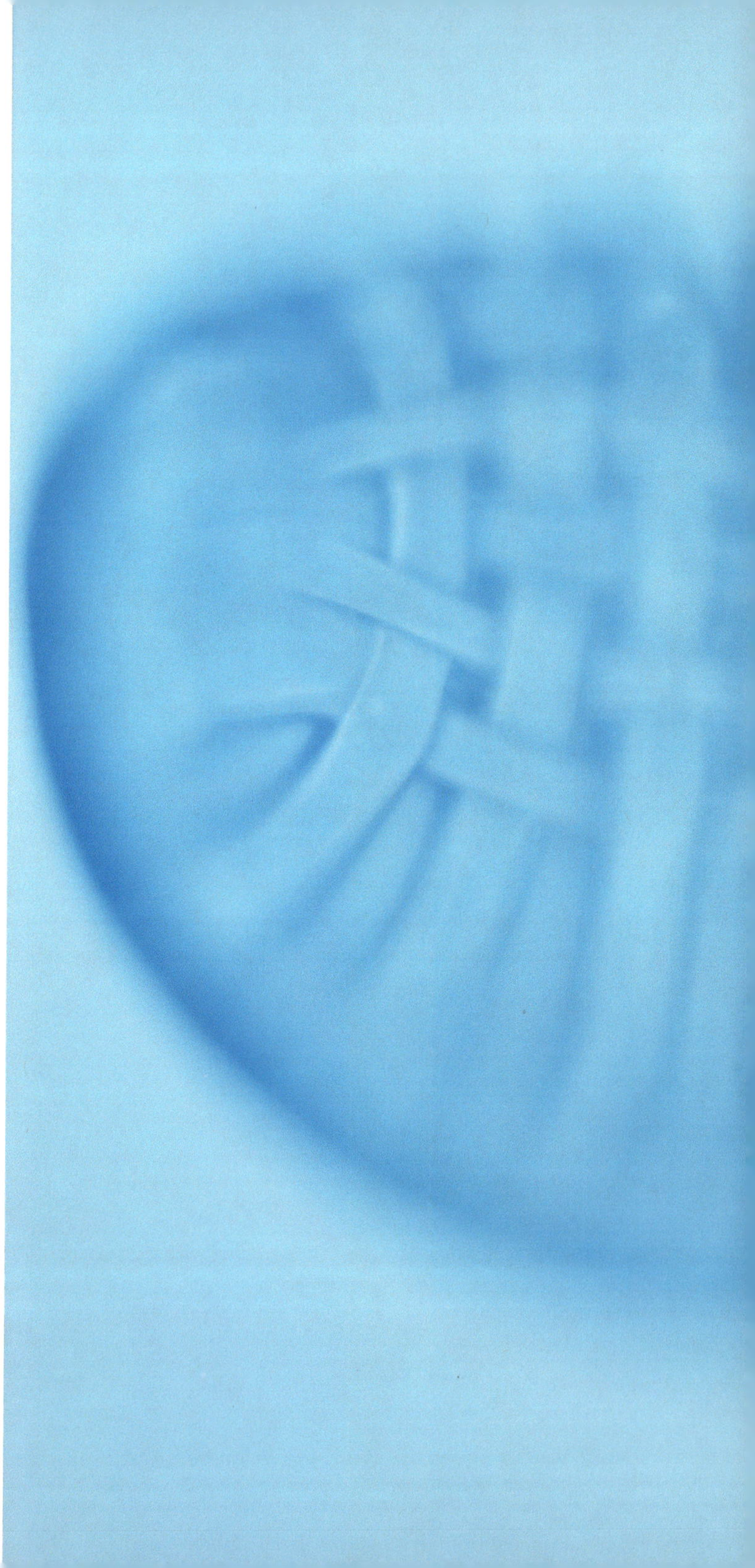

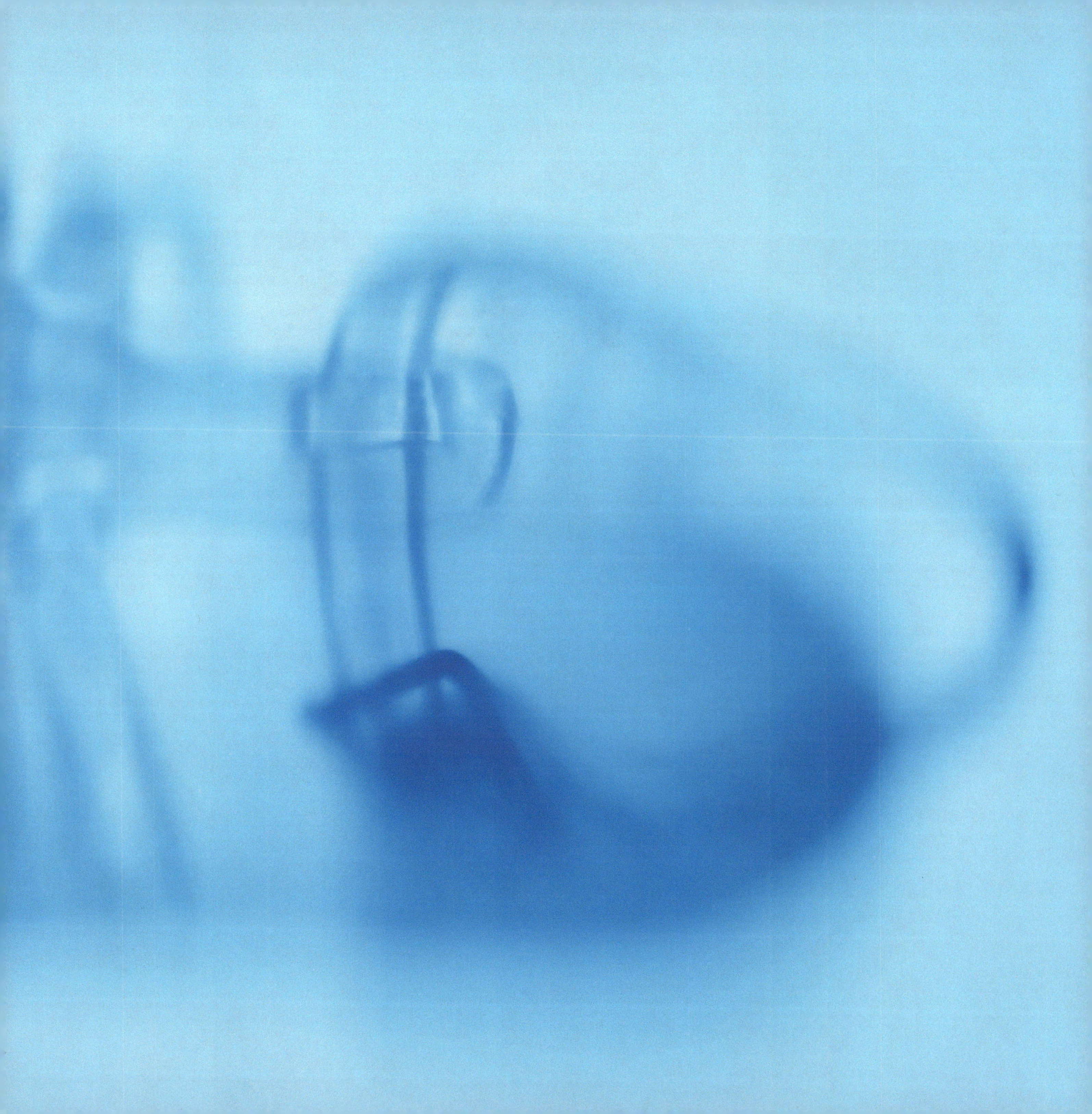

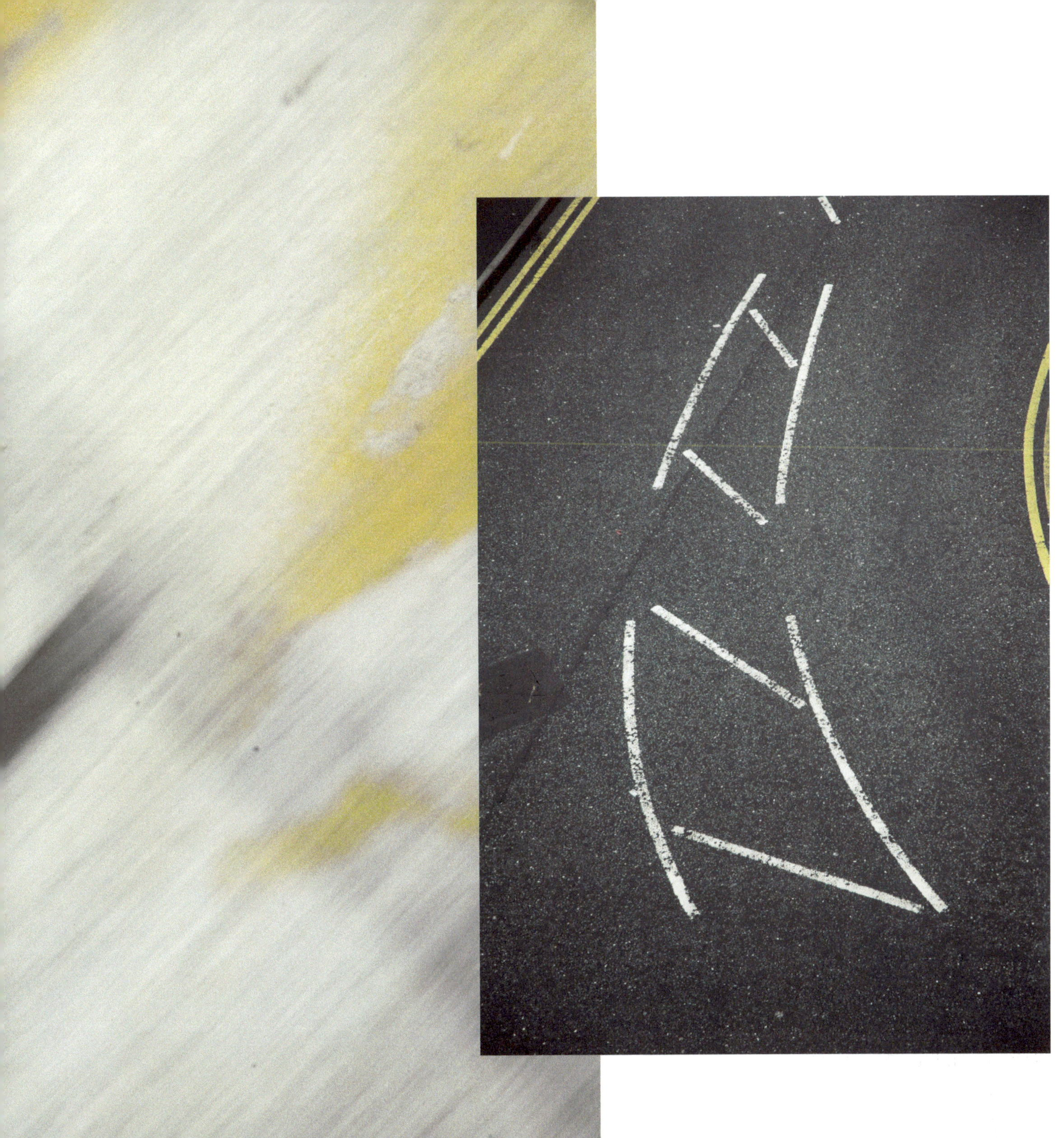

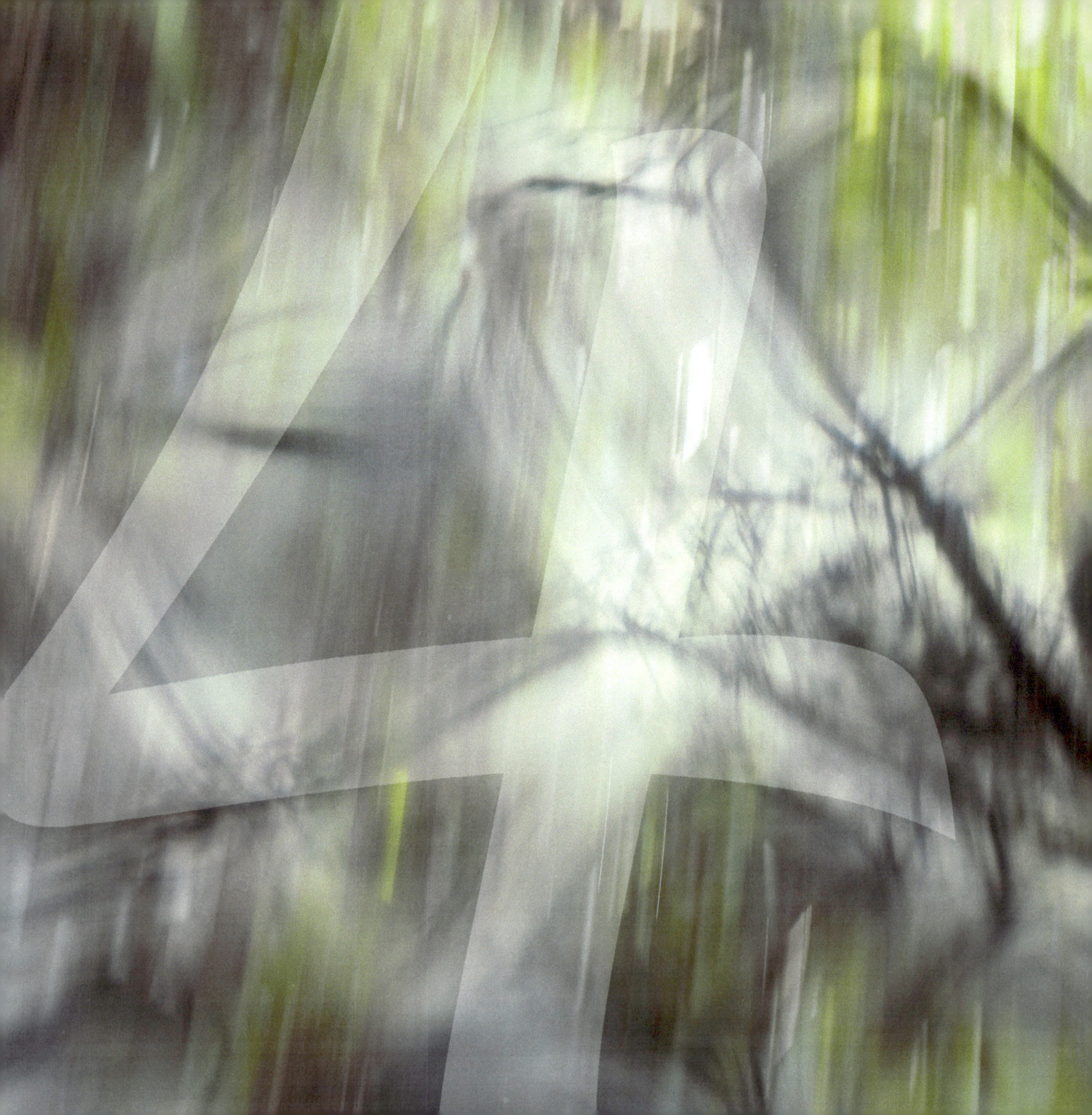
4

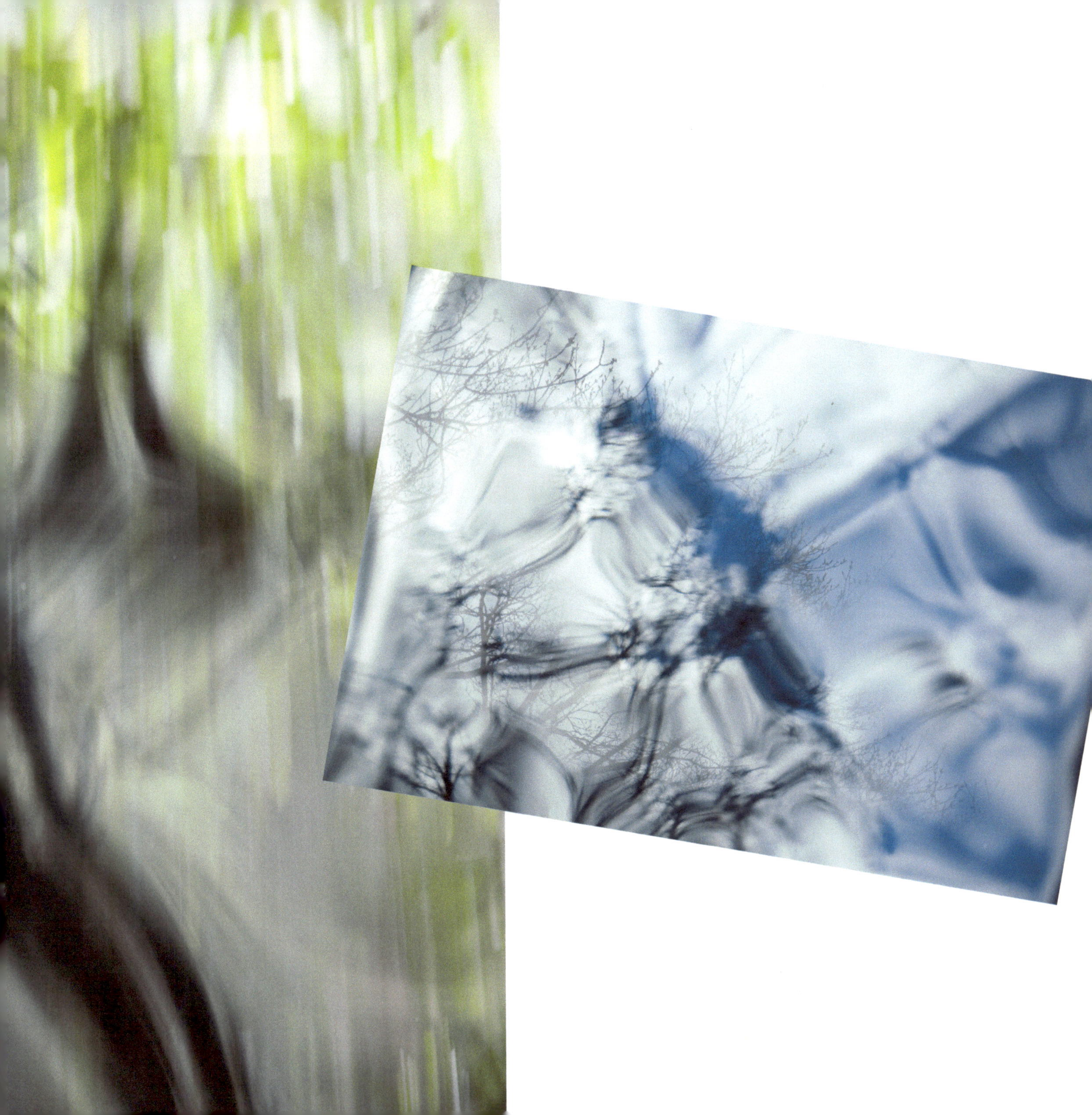

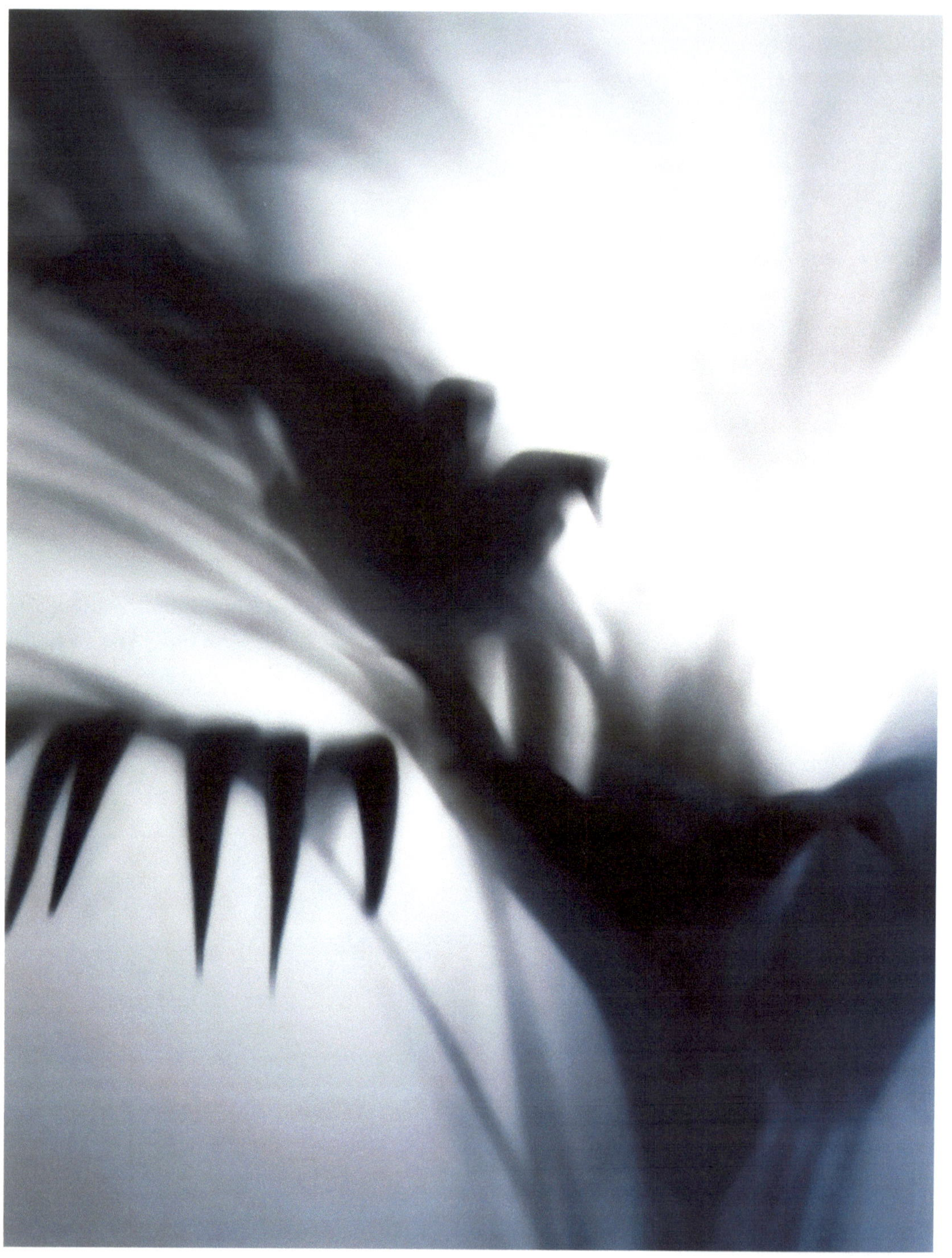

Misdirection is intended
to reveal something new
whilst hiding the obvious

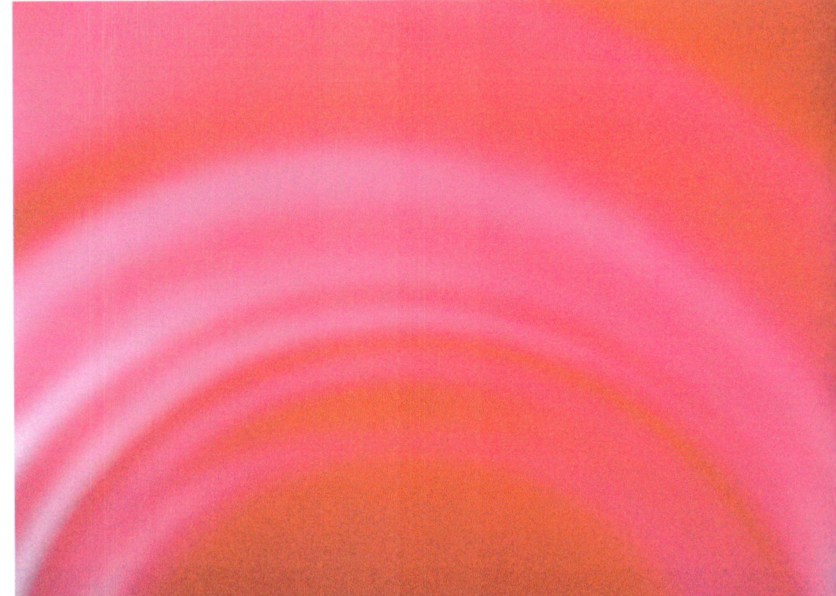

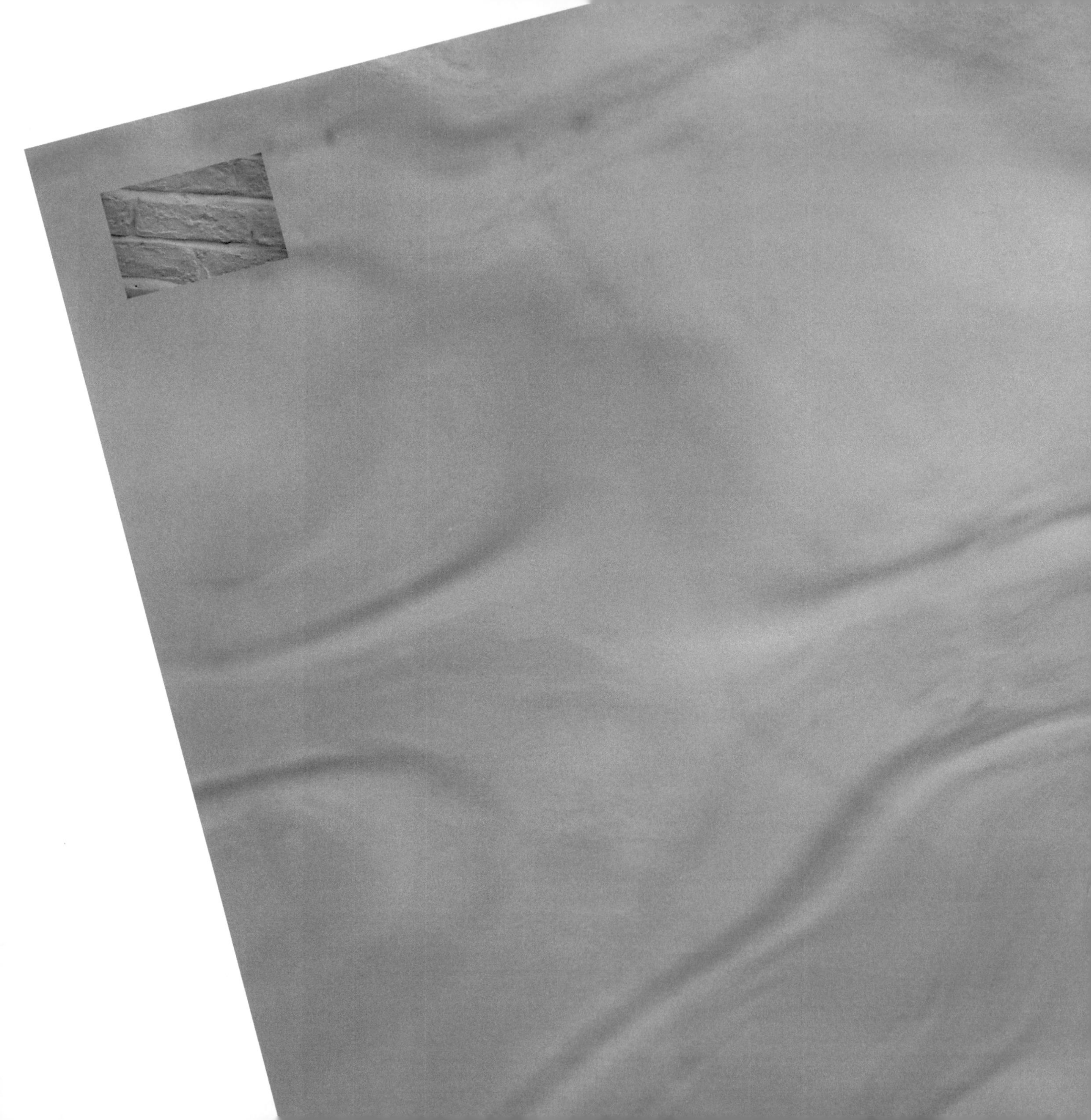

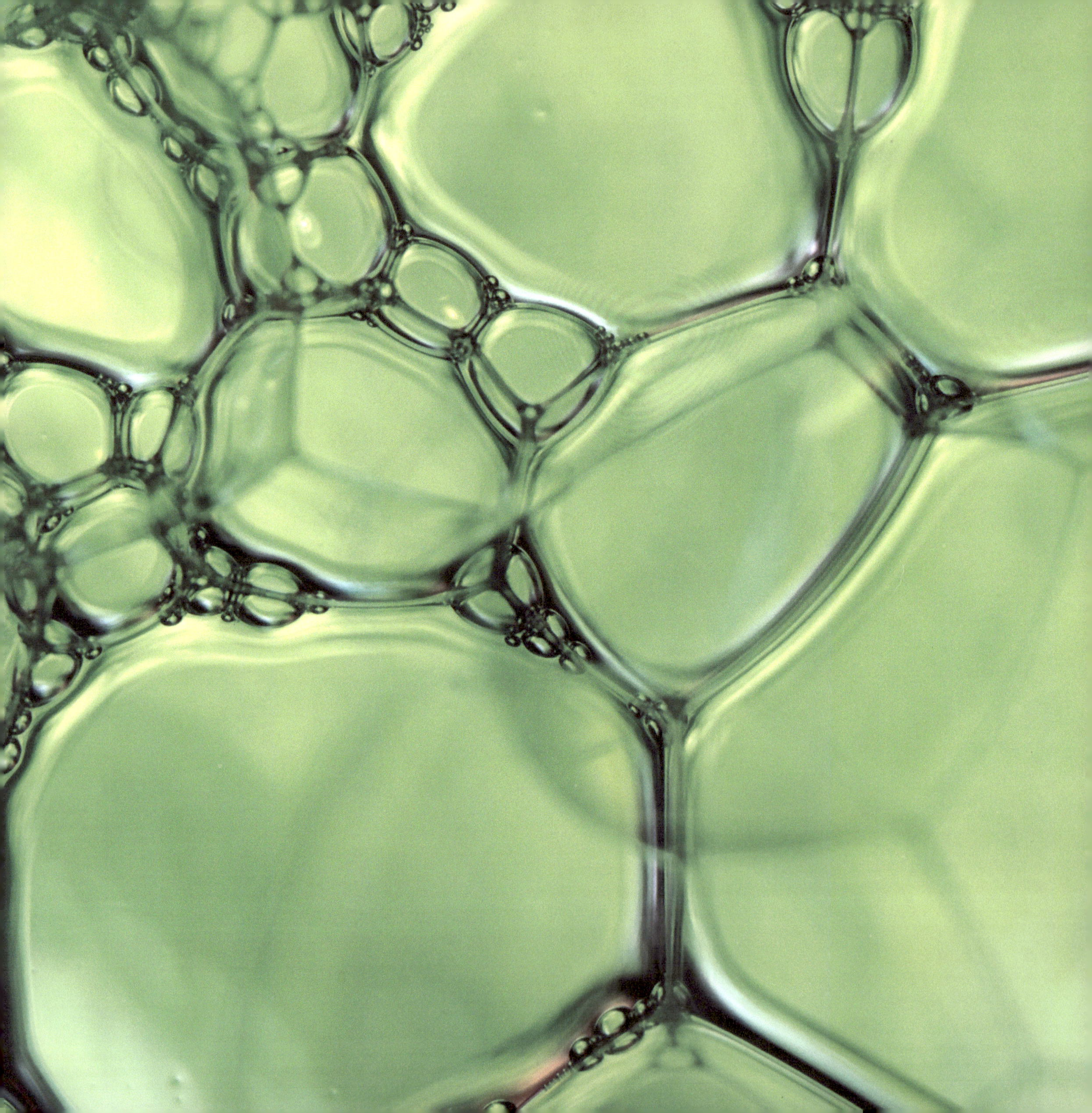

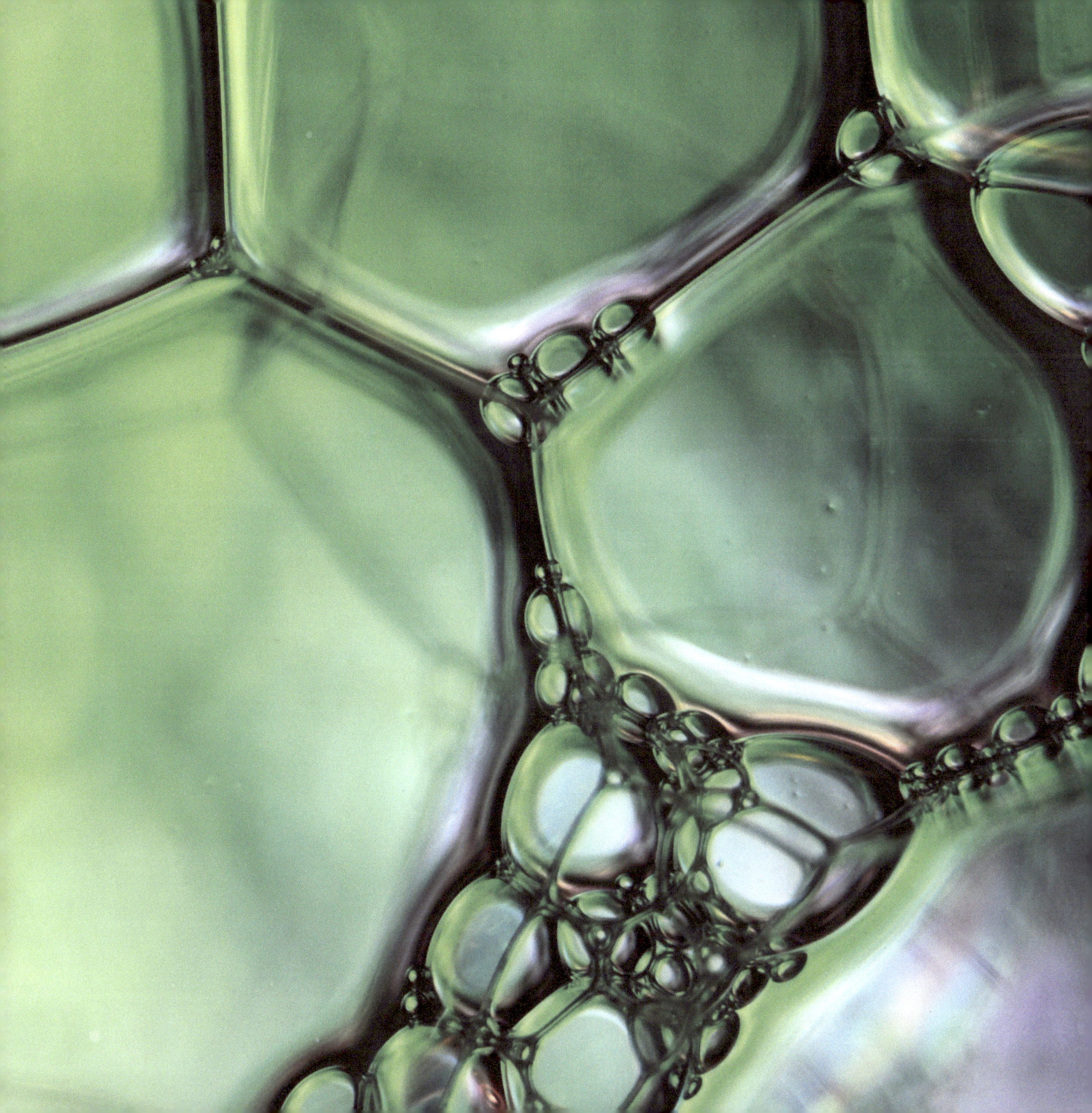

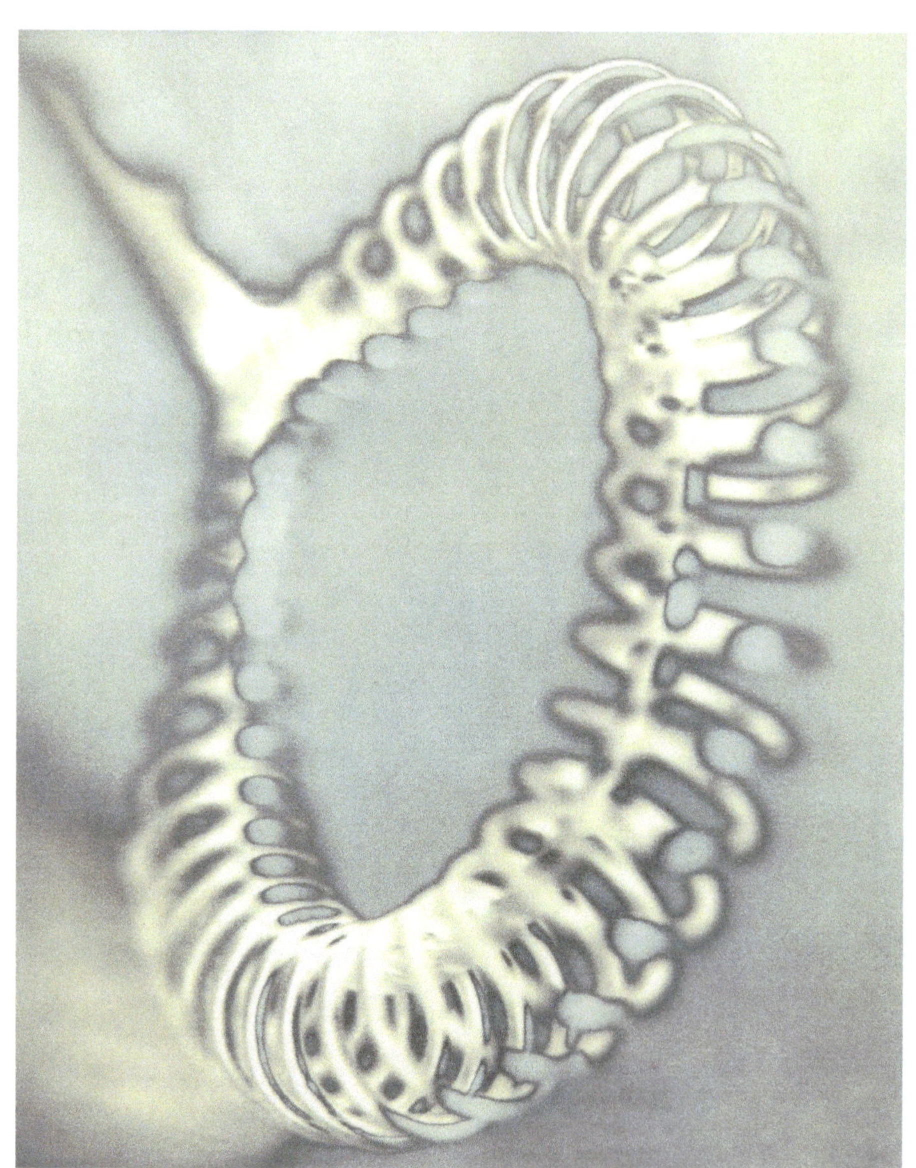

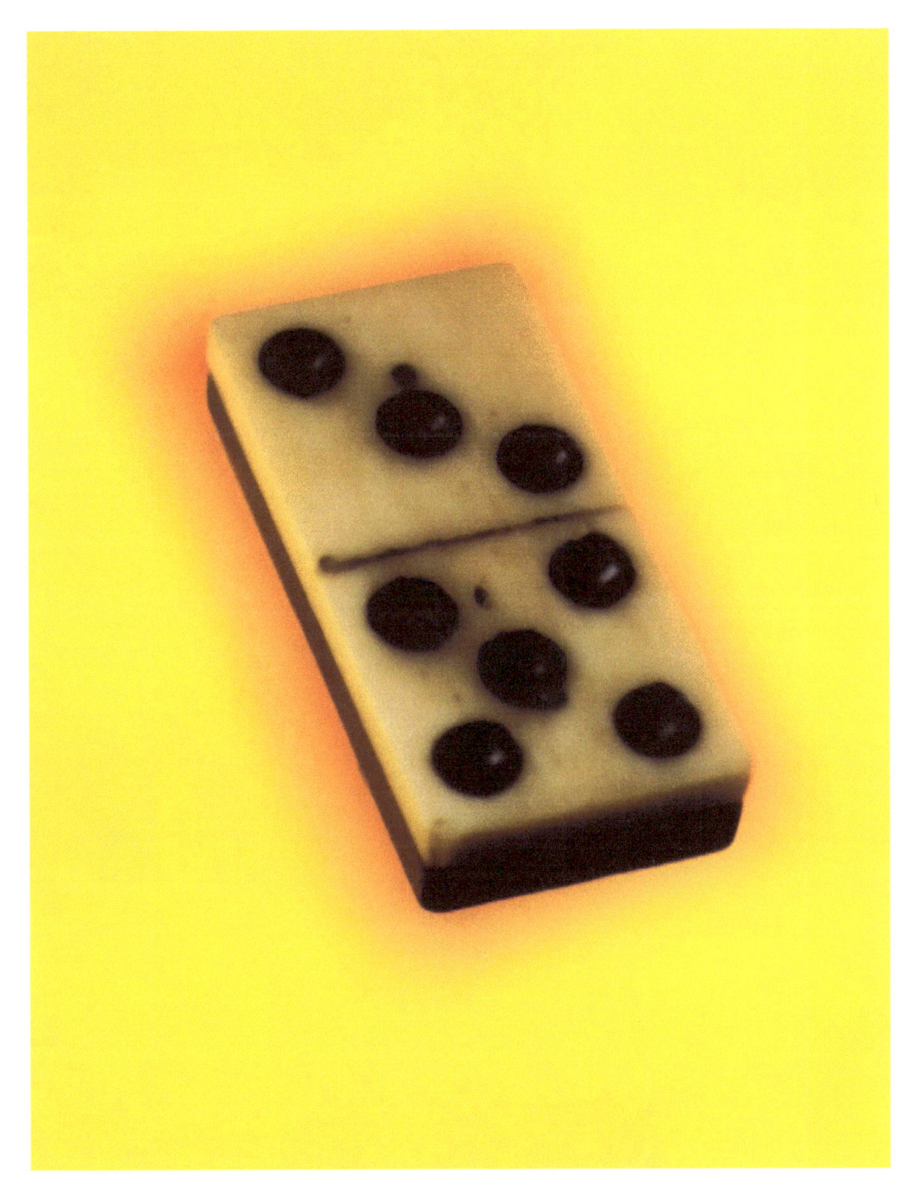

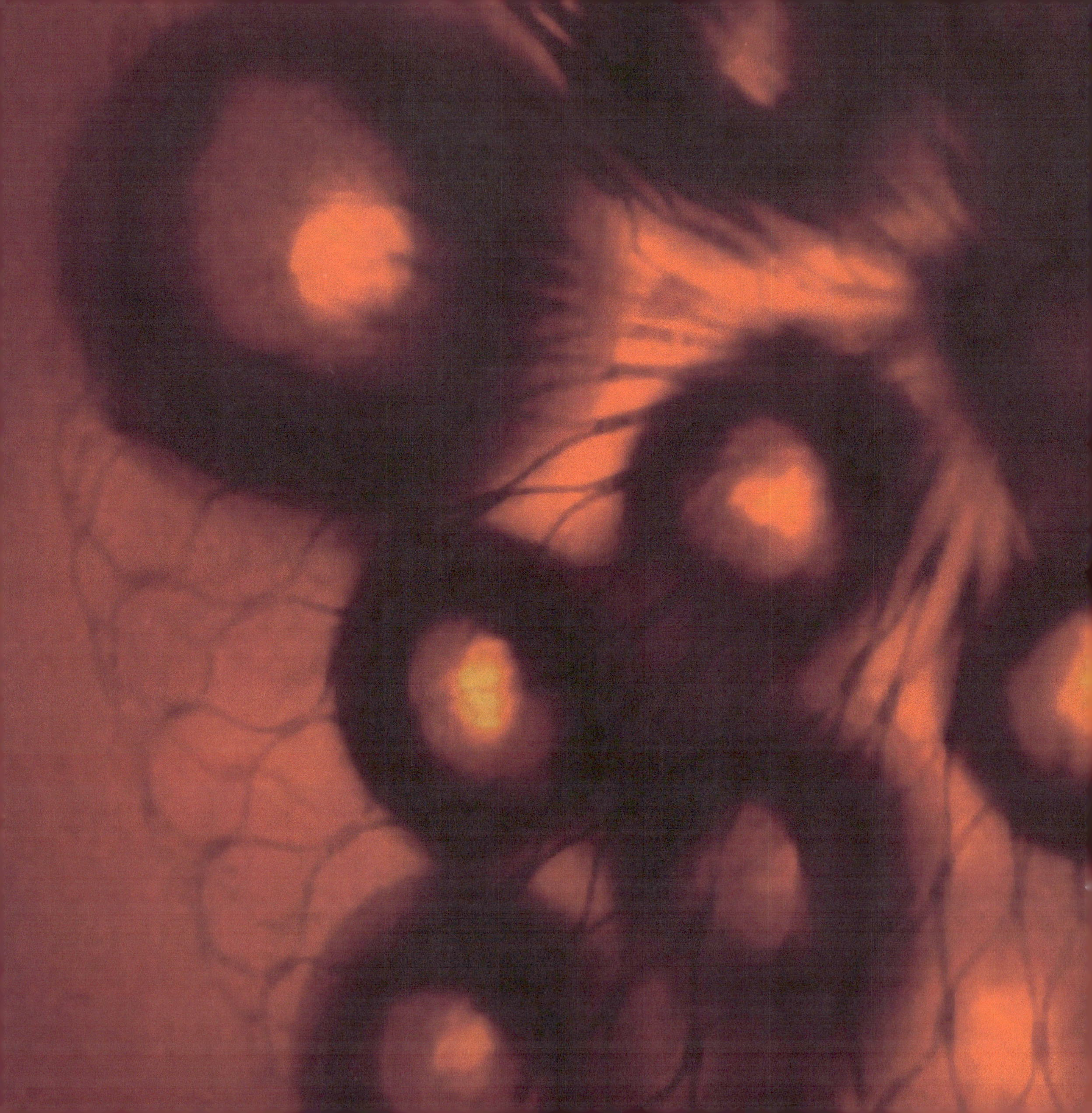

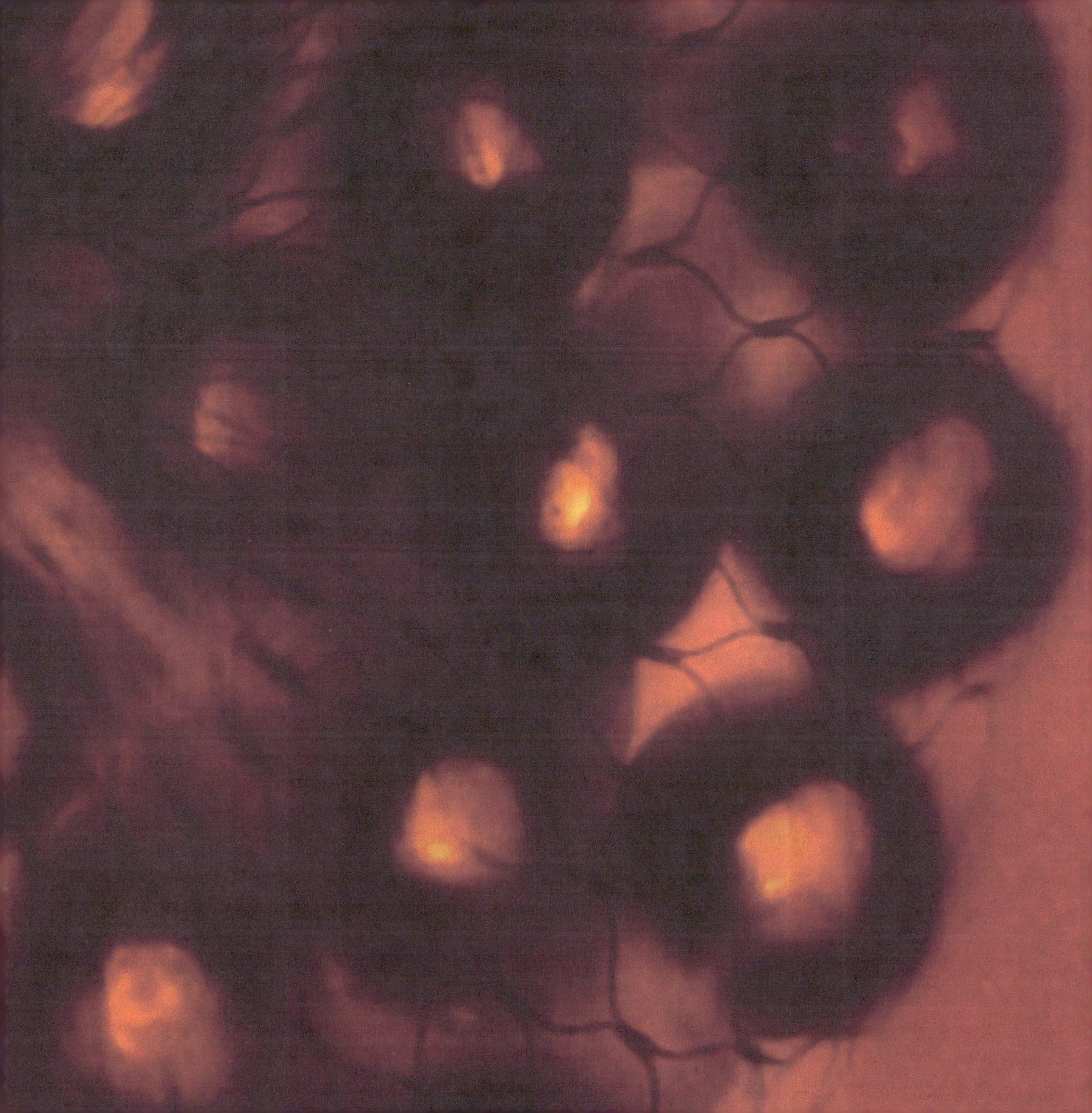

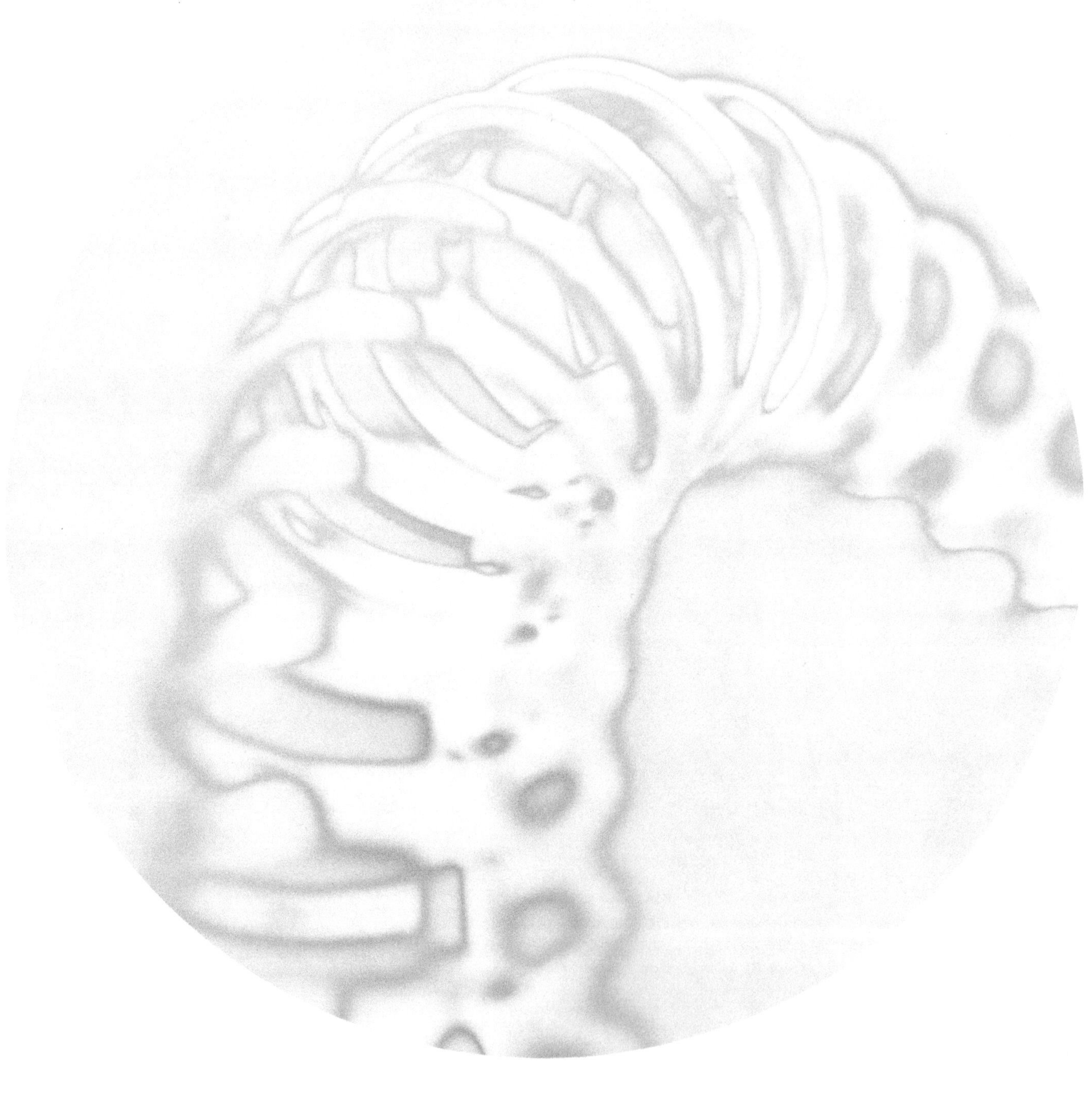

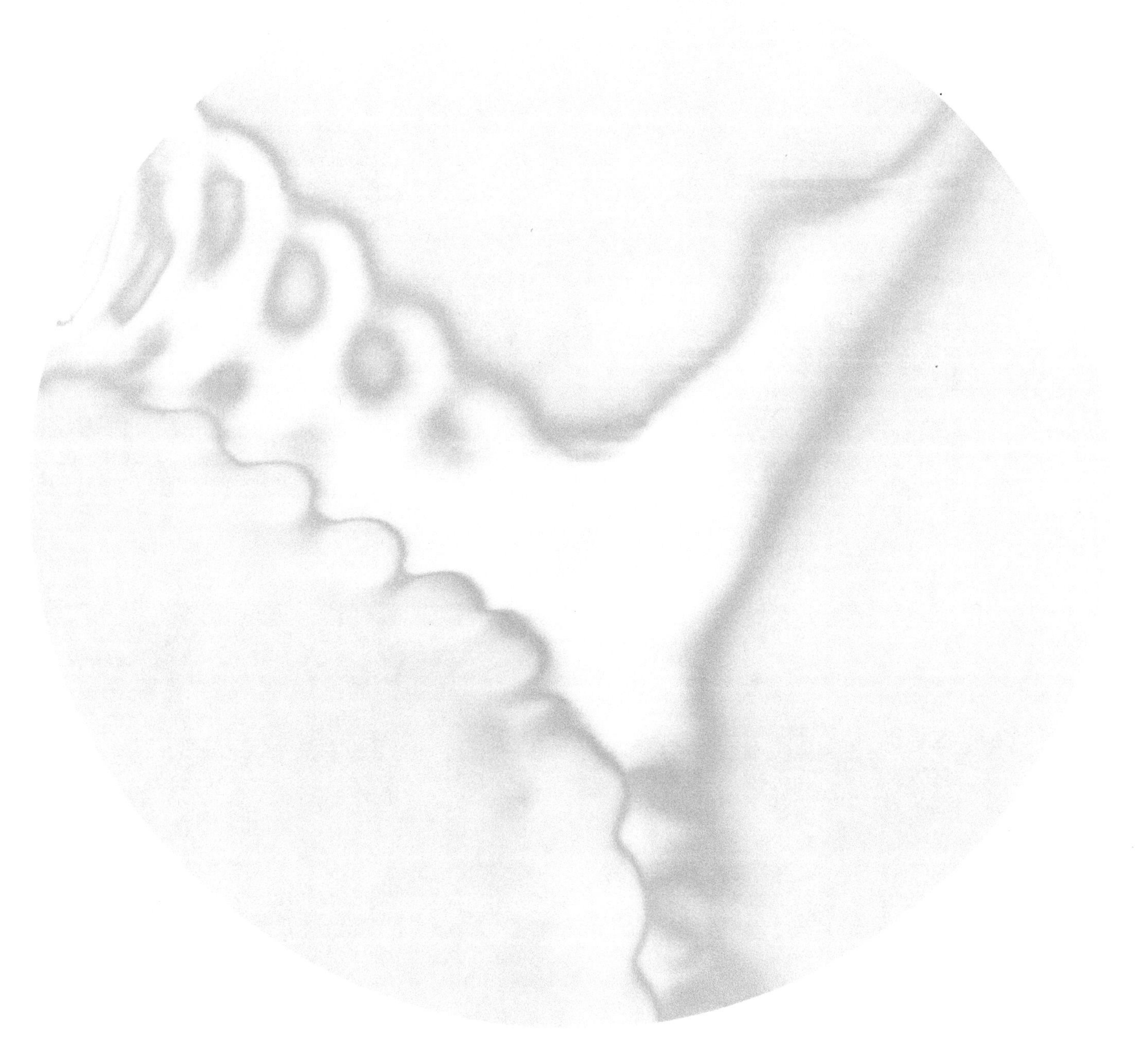

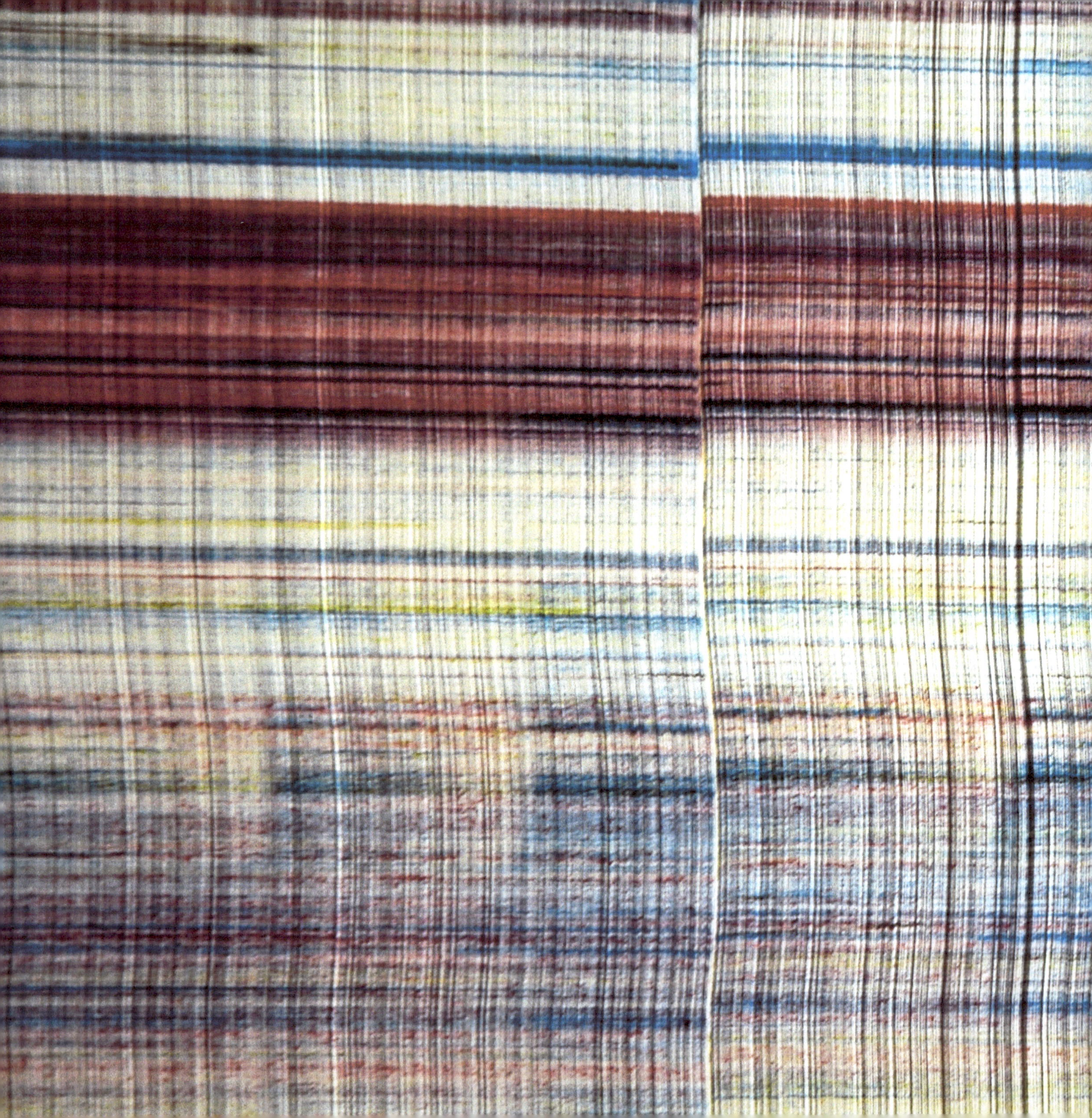

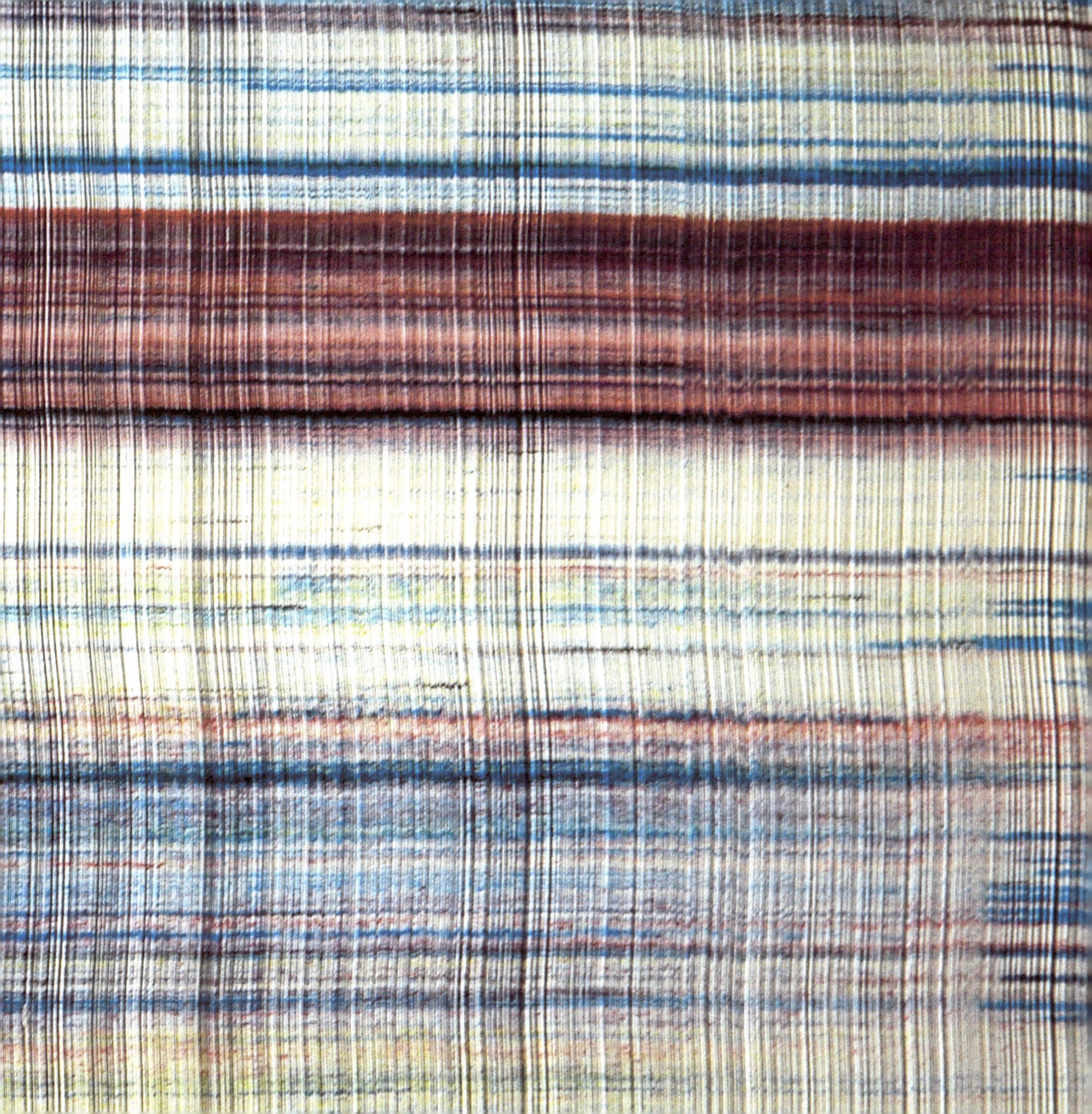

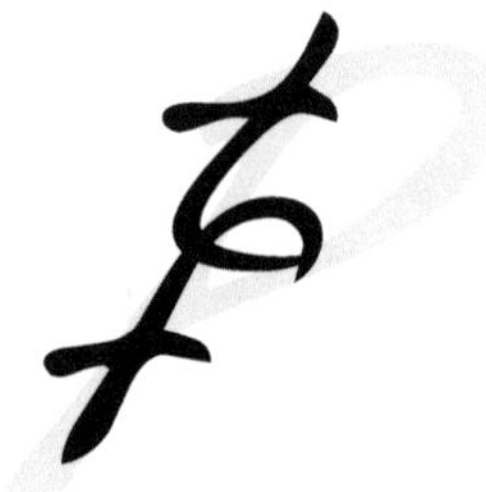

www.ingramcontent.com/pod-product-compliance
Lightning Source LLC
LaVergne TN
LVHW070203110826
845147LV00002B/489

* 9 7 8 0 9 5 7 6 8 2 0 0 9 *